Learn Your A B C 's

With Spoof

By
Mable Brothers Mullen
Illustrated by Jerry Mullen Jr.

SpeakLife
Publishing

Learn Your A B C 's

With Spoof

By
Mable Brothers Mullen
Illustrated by Jerry Mullen Jr.

ISBN: 978-0615831336
Published By SpeakLife Publishing

DEDICATION

In memory of my loving mother Lillian Brothers Mercer and sister Lynn B. Poyner.

ACKNOWLEDGEMENTS

I would like to thank God for blessing me with the gift of writing, and for my husband Jerry Mullen Jr., who did all the illustrations for my book. Honey, I thank you so much for that. To my sons Aaron and Donovan, I'm thankful for the countless times you've listened as I read my story. To my younger sisters; Denise Blocker, Melody De Vastey, and Angela Proctor, I thank you all for asking me to tell you stories when we were little girls growing up. To Mr.Mauricio Ortiz, Spanish Specialist who translated the alphabet word list. I would also like to thank all the staff of the local Office Max®.

Learn Your A B C 's

With Spoof

A is for the anthill that I dug up yesterday.

B is for a **b**ug that got in my way.

C is for the **c**at next-door that bit my tail.

D is for my doghouse beside my water pail.

E is for my floppy **e**ars that blow in the wind.

F is for my **f**amily that loves me wherever I've been.

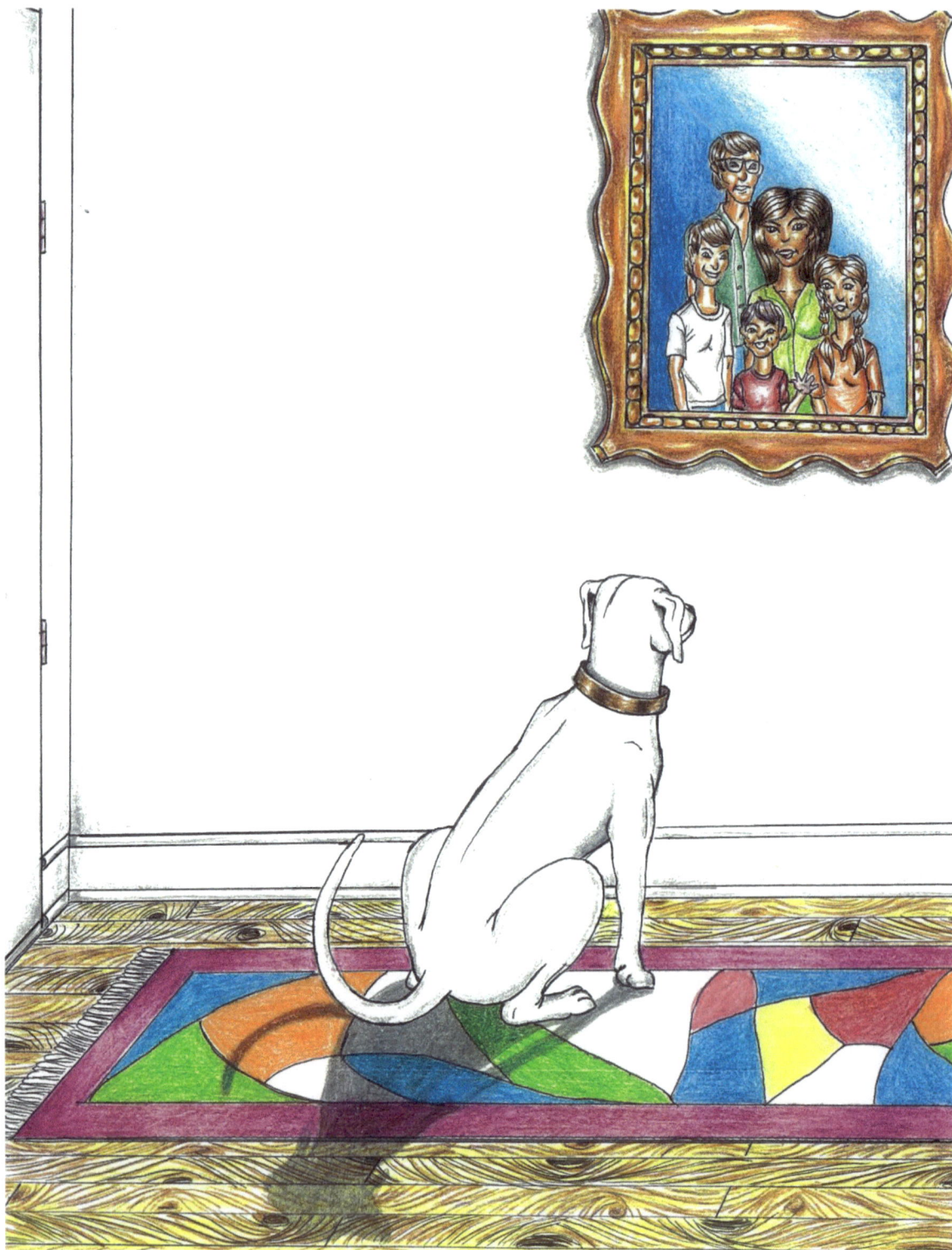

G is for a baby goat that eats from end to end.

H is for a mother **h**en whose chicks sleep in a pen.

I is for an itchy itch that I scratch all the time.

J is for a **jumbo jet** that leaves an airplane behind.

K is for a kind kid that helps me across the street.

L is for a lightning flash so bright that I cannot sleep.

M is for a little **m**ouse that lives inside our house.

N is for my **n**ose that's above my mouth.

O is for an **o**strich that I saw at the local zoo.

P is for a **p**arrot that can sing and play checkers too.

Q is for **q**uack **q**uack a sound you hear from a duck.

R is for **r**accoon that just got picked up by a truck.

S is for a **s**low **s**nail that leaves a **s**limy trail.

T is for a **t**urtle that hides inside its shell.

U is for **u**nicorn with wings that could fly.

V is for a **v**acuum that can suck up an ice cream pie.

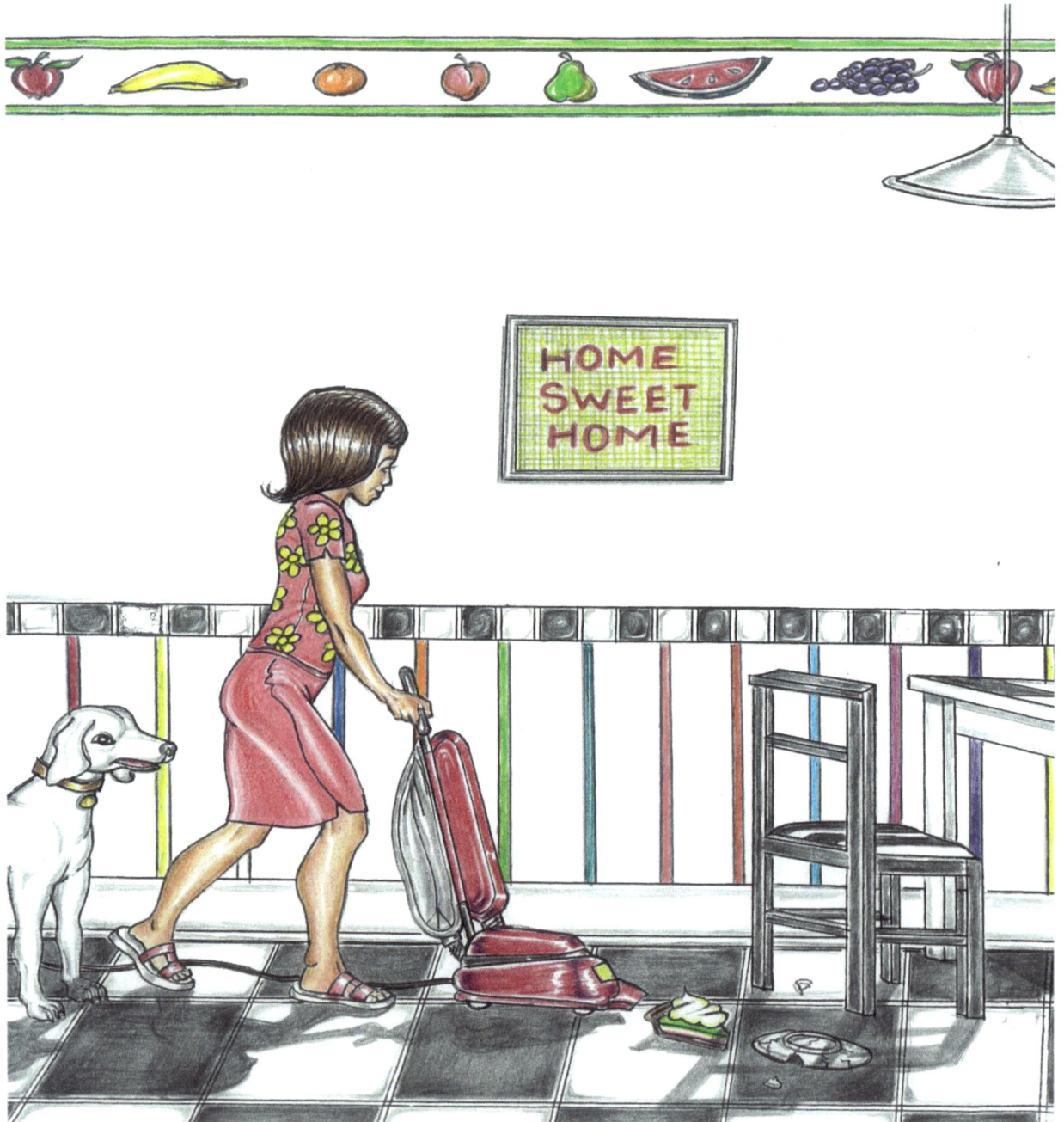

W is for a little brownish **w**orm on a fishing hook.

X is for x-ray for things that need a closer look.

Y is for the **y**olk of an egg sunny side up and you can eat them in bed.

Z is for **z**ebra with stripes black and white which make you dizzy if you stare with all your might.

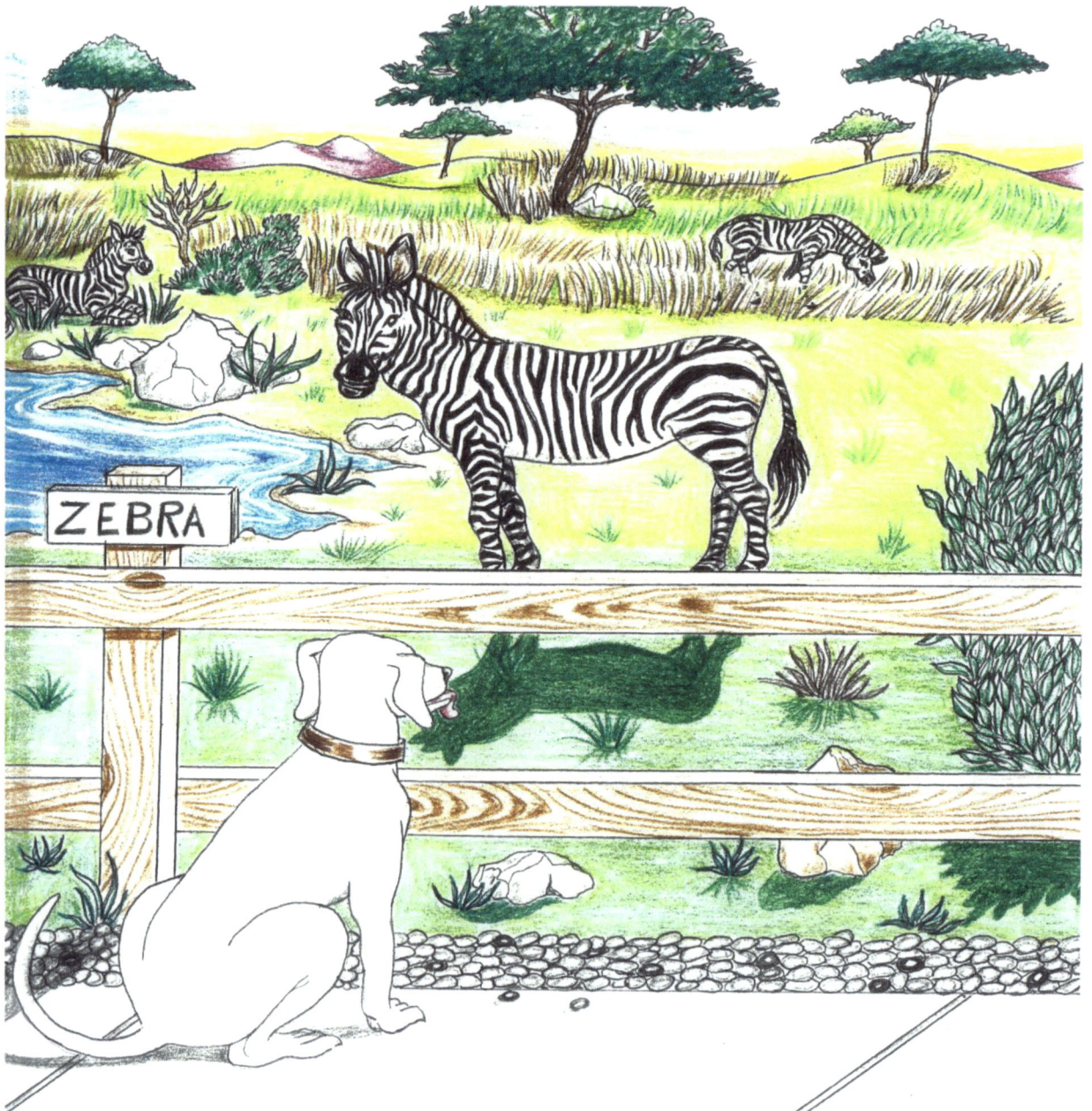

Alphabet Word List

English	Espanol
Anthill	Hormiguero
Bug	Bicho
Cat	Gato
Doghouse	Perrera
Ears	Orejas
Family	Familia
Goat	Cabra
Hen	Gallina
Itch	Comezon
Jet	Jet
Kid	Chico

Lightning	Relampago
Mouse	Raton
Nose	Nariz
Ostrich	Avestruz
Parrot	Loro
Quack	Cuack (Duck's quack)
Raccoon	Mapache
Snail	Caracol
Turtle	Tortuga
Unicorn	Unicornio
Vacuum	Aspiradora
Worm	Gusano
X-Ray	Rayso-X(Radiografia)
Yolk	Yema
Zebra	Zebra

ABOUT THE AUTHOR

Mable Brothers Mullen

Mable Brothers Mullen is the eleventh of fourteen children. As a girl growing up in North Carolina, she remembers when it was bed time and her mother would tuck Mable and her three younger sisters in and tell them, "Lights out, no talking and go to sleep." Being young girls and being very hot in that cramped bed, they could not sleep. So, every one of Mable's sisters would ask her to tell them a story. She was a very gifted story teller, and after telling one story her sisters would ask her to tell another. Often times, they would hear their mother call upstairs and say, "I said no talking. Ya'll better go to sleep." So Mable would tell her sisters that she would tell them two stories tomorrow night. All through school Mable's sisters would ask her to make up poems and other writing assignments for them. It wasn't until her late forties when she decided to write books. She wanted to write children's books because it took her back to her childhood days, when she would tell stories to her younger sisters in that One Big Bed.

Please Share With Us How Much You And Your Family Enjoyed
Learn Your ABC's With Spoof.

Contact Mable Brothers Mullen:
m.mullen57@yahoo.com

www.FamilyTheSeries.com
More Family-Friendly Books Are On The Way!